From the brilliant brain of

_____

daily journal

I have many things to write about this day. Just wait until you read what I have to say.

day

Mon
Tue   Sat
Wed   Sun
Thu
Fri

date

Jan   May   Sep
Feb   Jun   Oct
Mar   July   Nov
Apr   Aug   Dec

_____ / 20_____

feeling

Today this is me:

weather

Today outside is:

daily doodles

I like to draw. I will draw what I see. Today I saw all that you see.

daily to-do list

Good morning. Today is an awesome day. I have many fun things to do. Let's see!

1 ——————————————————— O
2 ——————————————————— O
3 ——————————————————— O
4 ——————————————————— O
5 ——————————————————— O
6 ——————————————————— O
7 ——————————————————— O
8 ——————————————————— O
9 ——————————————————— O
10 —————————————————— O
11 —————————————————— O
12 —————————————————— O
13 —————————————————— O
14 —————————————————— O
15 —————————————————— O
16 —————————————————— O
17 —————————————————— O
18 —————————————————— O
19 —————————————————— O
20 —————————————————— O
21 —————————————————— O
22 —————————————————— O
23 —————————————————— O
24 —————————————————— O

daily inspiration

Look what I discovered today! So many wonderful things I can do on another day.

to make   to eat   to find

to wear   to remember   to play

to ponder   to create   to see

to be   to visit   to match

daily expenses

Money is good. I work very hard. I want to know where it goes and how far.

Date	Amount	Balance

$5

$30

$3

$150

$200,000

From the brilliant brain of

_____

daily journal

I have many things to write about this day. Just wait until you read what I have to say.

day

Mon
Tue   Sat
Wed   Sun
Thu
Fri

date

Jan   May   Sep
Feb   Jun   Oct
Mar   July   Nov
Apr   Aug   Dec

_____ / 20_____

feeling

Today this is me:

weather

Today outside is:

daily doodles

I like to draw. I will draw what I see. Today I saw all that you see.

daily to-do list

Good morning. Today is an awesome day. I have many fun things to do. Let's see!

1. ⭘
2. ⭘
3. ⭘
4. ⭘
5. ⭘
6. ⭘
7. ⭘
8. ⭘
9. ⭘
10. ⭘
11. ⭘
12. ⭘
13. ⭘
14. ⭘
15. ⭘
16. ⭘
17. ⭘
18. ⭘
19. ⭘
20. ⭘
21. ⭘
22. ⭘
23. ⭘
24. ⭘

daily inspiration

Look what I discovered today! So many wonderful things I can do on another day.

to make   to eat   to find

to wear   to remember   to play

to ponder   to create   to see

to be   to visit   to match

daily expenses

Money is good. I work very hard. I want to know where it goes and how far.

Date	Amount	Balance

$5

$30

$3

$150

$200,000

From the brilliant brain of

_____

daily journal

I have many things to write about this day. Just wait until you read what I have to say.

day
Mon
Tue   Sat
Wed   Sun
Thu
Fri

date
Jan   May   Sep
Feb   Jun   Oct
Mar   July   Nov
Apr   Aug   Dec

_____ / 20_____

feeling
Today this is me:

weather
Today outside is:

daily doodles

I like to draw. I will draw what I see. Today I saw all that you see.

daily to-do list

Good morning. Today is an awesome day. I have many fun things to do. Let's see!

1
2
3
4
5
6
7
8
9
10
11
12
13
14
15
16
17
18
19
20
21
22
23
24

daily inspiration

Look what I discovered today! So many wonderful things I can do on another day.

to make   to eat   to find

to wear   to remember   to play

to ponder   to create   to see

to be   to visit   to match

daily expenses

Money is good. I work very hard. I want to know where it goes and how far.

Date	Amount	Balance

$5

$30

$3

$150

$200,000

From the brilliant brain of

_____

daily journal

I have many things to write about this day. Just wait until you read what I have to say.

day

Mon
Tue   Sat
Wed   Sun
Thu
Fri

date

Jan   May   Sep
Feb   Jun   Oct
Mar   July   Nov
Apr   Aug   Dec

_____ / 20 _____

feeling

Today this is me:

weather

Today outside is:

daily doodles

I like to draw. I will draw what I see. Today I saw all that you see.

daily to-do list

Good morning. Today is an awesome day. I have many fun things to do. Let's see!

1
2
3
4
5
6
7
8
9
10
11
12
13
14
15
16
17
18
19
20
21
22
23
24

daily inspiration

Look what I discovered today! So many wonderful things I can do on another day.

to make　　to eat　　to find

to wear　　to remember　　to play

to ponder　　to create　　to see

to be　　to visit　　to match

daily expenses

Money is good. I work very hard. I want to know where it goes and how far.

Date	Amount	Balance

$5

$30

$3

$150

$200,000

From the brilliant brain of

_____

daily journal

I have many things to write about this day. Just wait until you read what I have to say.

day

Mon
Tue   Sat
Wed   Sun
Thu
Fri

date

Jan   May   Sep
Feb   Jun   Oct
Mar   July   Nov
Apr   Aug   Dec

_____ / 20_____

feeling

Today this is me:

weather

Today outside is:

daily doodles

I like to draw. I will draw what I see. Today I saw all that you see.

daily to-do list

Good morning. Today is an awesome day. I have many fun things to do. Let's see!

1. ☐
2. ☐
3. ☐
4. ☐
5. ☐
6. ☐
7. ☐
8. ☐
9. ☐
10. ☐
11. ☐
12. ☐
13. ☐
14. ☐
15. ☐
16. ☐
17. ☐
18. ☐
19. ☐
20. ☐
21. ☐
22. ☐
23. ☐
24. ☐

daily inspiration

Look what I discovered today! So many wonderful things I can do on another day.

to make   to eat   to find

to wear   to remember   to play

to ponder   to create   to see

to be   to visit   to match

daily expenses

Money is good. I work very hard. I want to know where it goes and how far.

Date	Amount	Balance

$5

$30

$3

$150

$200,000

From the brilliant brain of

_____

daily journal

I have many things to write about this day. Just wait until you read what I have to say.

day

Mon
Tue   Sat
Wed   Sun
Thu
Fri

date

Jan   May   Sep
Feb   Jun   Oct
Mar   July   Nov
Apr   Aug   Dec

_____ / 20_____

feeling

Today this is me:

weather

Today outside is:

daily doodles

I like to draw. I will draw what I see. Today I saw all that you see.

daily to-do list

Good morning. Today is an awesome day. I have many fun things to do. Let's see!

1. ○
2. ○
3. ○
4. ○
5. ○
6. ○
7. ○
8. ○
9. ○
10. ○
11. ○
12. ○
13. ○
14. ○
15. ○
16. ○
17. ○
18. ○
19. ○
20. ○
21. ○
22. ○
23. ○
24. ○

daily inspiration

Look what I discovered today! So many wonderful things I can do on another day.

to make   to eat   to find

to wear   to remember   to play

to ponder   to create   to see

to be   to visit   to match

daily expenses

Money is good. I work very hard. I want to know where it goes and how far.

Date	Amount	Balance

$5

$30

$3

$-150

200,000

From the brilliant brain of

_____

daily journal

I have many things to write about this day. Just wait until you read what I have to say.

day
Mon
Tue   Sat
Wed   Sun
Thu
Fri

date
Jan   May   Sep
Feb   Jun   Oct
Mar   July Nov
Apr   Aug   Dec

_____ / 20_____

feeling
Today this is me:

weather
Today outside is:

daily doodles

I like to draw. I will draw what I see. Today I saw all that you see.

daily to-do list

Good morning. Today is an awesome day. I have many fun things to do. Let's see!

1
2
3
4
5
6
7
8
9
10
11
12
13
14
15
16
17
18
19
20
21
22
23
24

daily inspiration

Look what I discovered today! So many wonderful things I can do on another day.

to make   to eat   to find

to wear   to remember   to play

to ponder   to create   to see

to be   to visit   to match

daily expenses

Money is good. I work very hard. I want to know where it goes and how far.

Date	Amount	Balance

$5

$30

$3

$150

$200,000

From the brilliant brain of

_____

daily journal

I have many things to write about this day. Just wait until you read what I have to say.

day

Mon
Tue   Sat
Wed   Sun
Thu
Fri

date

Jan   May   Sep
Feb   Jun   Oct
Mar   July   Nov
Apr   Aug   Dec

_____ / 20 _____

feeling

Today this is me:

weather

Today outside is:

daily doodles

I like to draw. I will draw what I see. Today I saw all that you see.

daily to-do list

Good morning. Today is an awesome day. I have many fun things to do. Let's see!

1. ○
2. ○
3. ○
4. ○
5. ○
6. ○
7. ○
8. ○
9. ○
10. ○
11. ○
12. ○
13. ○
14. ○
15. ○
16. ○
17. ○
18. ○
19. ○
20. ○
21. ○
22. ○
23. ○
24. ○

daily expenses

Money is good. I work very hard. I want to know where it goes and how far.

Date	Amount	Balance

$5

$30

$3

$150

$200,000

From the brilliant brain of

_____

daily journal

I have many things to write about this day. Just wait until you read what I have to say.

day
Mon
Tue Sat
Wed Sun
Thu
Fri

date
Jan	May	Sep
Feb	Jun	Oct
Mar	July	Nov
Apr	Aug	Dec

_____ / 20 _____

feeling
Today this is me:

weather
Today outside is:

daily doodles

I like to draw. I will draw what I see. Today I saw all that you see.

daily to-do list

Good morning. Today is an awesome day. I have many fun things to do. Let's see!

1
2
3
4
5
6
7
8
9
10
11
12
13
14
15
16
17
18
19
20
21
22
23
24

daily inspiration

Look what I discovered today! So many wonderful things I can do on another day.

to make   to eat   to find

to wear   to remember   to play

to ponder   to create   to see

to be   to visit   to match

daily expenses

Money is good. I work very hard. I want to know where it goes and how far.

Date	Amount	Balance

$5

$30

$3

$150

$200,000

From the brilliant brain of

_____

daily journal

I have many things to write about this day. Just wait until you read what I have to say.

day
Mon
Tue Sat
Wed Sun
Thu
Fri

date
Jan May Sep
Feb Jun Oct
Mar July Nov
Apr Aug Dec

_____ / 20_____

feeling
Today this is me:

weather
Today outside is:

daily doodles

I like to draw. I will draw what I see. Today I saw all that you see.

daily to-do list

Good morning. Today is an awesome day. I have many fun things to do. Let's see!

1. ○
2. ○
3. ○
4. ○
5. ○
6. ○
7. ○
8. ○
9. ○
10. ○
11. ○
12. ○
13. ○
14. ○
15. ○
16. ○
17. ○
18. ○
19. ○
20. ○
21. ○
22. ○
23. ○
24. ○

daily inspiration

Look what I discovered today! So many wonderful things I can do on another day.

to make   to eat   to find

to wear   to remember   to play

to ponder   to create   to see

to be   to visit   to match

daily expenses

Money is good. I work very hard. I want to know where it goes and how far.

Date	Amount	Balance

$5

$30

$3

$150

$200,000

From the brilliant brain of

_____

daily journal

I have many things to write about this day. Just wait until you read what I have to say.

day

Mon
Tue   Sat
Wed   Sun
Thu
Fri

date

Jan   May   Sep
Feb   Jun   Oct
Mar   July   Nov
Apr   Aug   Dec

_____ / 20_____

feeling

Today this is me:

weather

Today outside is:

daily doodles

I like to draw. I will draw what I see. Today I saw all that you see.

daily to-do list

Good morning. Today is an awesome day. I have many fun things to do. Let's see!

1
2
3
4
5
6
7
8
9
10
11
12
13
14
15
16
17
18
19
20
21
22
23
24

daily inspiration

Look what I discovered today! So many wonderful things I can do on another day.

to make   to eat   to find

to wear   to remember   to play

to ponder   to create   to see

to be   to visit   to match

daily expenses

Money is good. I work very hard. I want to know where it goes and how far.

Date	Amount	Balance

$5

$30

$3

$150

$200,000

From the brilliant brain of

_____

daily journal

I have many things to write about this day. Just wait until you read what I have to say.

day

Mon
Tue   Sat
Wed   Sun
Thu
Fri

date

Jan   May   Sep
Feb   Jun   Oct
Mar   July   Nov
Apr   Aug   Dec

_____ / 20 _____

feeling

Today this is me:

weather

Today outside is:

daily doodles

I like to draw. I will draw what I see. Today I saw all that you see.

daily to-do list

Good morning. Today is an awesome day. I have many fun things to do. Let's see!

1. ⚪
2. ⚪
3. ⚪
4. ⚪
5. ⚪
6. ⚪
7. ⚪
8. ⚪
9. ⚪
10. ⚪
11. ⚪
12. ⚪
13. ⚪
14. ⚪
15. ⚪
16. ⚪
17. ⚪
18. ⚪
19. ⚪
20. ⚪
21. ⚪
22. ⚪
23. ⚪
24. ⚪

daily inspiration

Look what I discovered today! So many wonderful things I can do on another day.

to make   to eat   to find

to wear   to remember   to play

to ponder   to create   to see

to be   to visit   to match

daily expenses

Money is good. I work very hard. I want to know where it goes and how far.

Date	Amount	Balance

$5

$30

$3

$150

$200,000

From the brilliant brain of

_____

daily journal

I have many things to write about this day. Just wait until you read what I have to say.

day

Mon
Tue   Sat
Wed   Sun
Thu
Fri

date

Jan   May   Sep
Feb   Jun   Oct
Mar   July   Nov
Apr   Aug   Dec

_____ / 20 _____

feeling

Today this is me:

weather

Today outside is:

daily doodles

I like to draw. I will draw what I see. Today I saw all that you see.

daily to-do list

Good morning. Today is an awesome day. I have many fun things to do. Let's see!

1. ○
2. ○
3. ○
4. ○
5. ○
6. ○
7. ○
8. ○
9. ○
10. ○
11. ○
12. ○
13. ○
14. ○
15. ○
16. ○
17. ○
18. ○
19. ○
20. ○
21. ○
22. ○
23. ○
24. ○

daily inspiration

Look what I discovered today! So many wonderful things I can do on another day.

to make   to eat   to find

to wear   to remember   to play

to ponder   to create   to see

to be   to visit   to match

daily expenses

Money is good. I work very hard. I want to know where it goes and how far.

Date	Amount	Balance

$5

$30

$3

$150

200,000

From the brilliant brain of

_____

daily journal

I have many things to write about this day. Just wait until you read what I have to say.

day	date	feeling	weather
Mon	Jan May Sep	Today this is me:	Today outside is:
Tue Sat	Feb Jun Oct		
Wed Sun	Mar July Nov		
Thu	Apr Aug Dec		
Fri	____ / 20 ____		

daily doodles

I like to draw. I will draw what I see. Today I saw all that you see.

daily to-do list

Good morning. Today is an awesome day. I have many fun things to do. Let's see!

1.   ○
2.   ○
3.   ○
4.   ○
5.   ○
6.   ○
7.   ○
8.   ○
9.   ○
10.   ○
11.   ○
12.   ○
13.   ○
14.   ○
15.   ○
16.   ○
17.   ○
18.   ○
19.   ○
20.   ○
21.   ○
22.   ○
23.   ○
24.   ○

daily inspiration

Look what I discovered today! So many wonderful things I can do on another day.

to make   to eat   to find

to wear   to remember   to play

to ponder   to create   to see

to be   to visit   to match

daily expenses

Money is good. I work very hard. I want to know where it goes and how far.

Date	Amount	Balance

$5

$30

$3

$150

$200,000

From the brilliant brain of

_____

daily journal

I have many things to write about this day. Just wait until you read what I have to say.

day

Mon
Tue   Sat
Wed   Sun
Thu
Fri

date

Jan   May   Sep
Feb   Jun   Oct
Mar   July   Nov
Apr   Aug   Dec

_____ / 20_____

feeling

Today this is me:

weather

Today outside is:

daily doodles

I like to draw. I will draw what I see. Today I saw all that you see.

daily to-do list

Good morning. Today is an awesome day. I have many fun things to do. Let's see!

1 ○
2 ○
3 ○
4 ○
5 ○
6 ○
7 ○
8 ○
9 ○
10 ○
11 ○
12 ○
13 ○
14 ○
15 ○
16 ○
17 ○
18 ○
19 ○
20 ○
21 ○
22 ○
23 ○
24 ○

daily inspiration

Look what I discovered today! So many wonderful things I can do on another day.

to make   to eat   to find

to wear   to remember   to play

to ponder   to create   to see

to be   to visit   to match

daily expenses

Money is good. I work very hard. I want to know where it goes and how far.

Date	Amount	Balance

$5

$30

$3

$150

$200,000

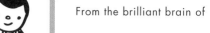

From the brilliant brain of

_____

daily journal

I have many things to write about this day. Just wait until you read what I have to say.

day
Mon
Tue   Sat
Wed   Sun
Thu
Fri

date
Jan   May   Sep
Feb   Jun   Oct
Mar   July   Nov
Apr   Aug   Dec

_____ / 20 _____

feeling
Today this is me:

weather
Today outside is:

daily doodles

I like to draw. I will draw what I see. Today I saw all that you see.

daily to-do list

Good morning. Today is an awesome day. I have many fun things to do. Let's see!

1. ○
2. ○
3. ○
4. ○
5. ○
6. ○
7. ○
8. ○
9. ○
10. ○
11. ○
12. ○
13. ○
14. ○
15. ○
16. ○
17. ○
18. ○
19. ○
20. ○
21. ○
22. ○
23. ○
24. ○

daily inspiration

Look what I discovered today! So many wonderful things I can do on another day.

to make   to eat   to find

to wear   to remember   to play

to ponder   to create   to see

to be   to visit   to match

daily expenses

Money is good. I work very hard. I want to know where it goes and how far.

Date	Amount	Balance

$5

$30

$3

$150

$200,000

From the brilliant brain of

_____

daily journal

I have many things to write about this day. Just wait until you read what I have to say.

day	date	feeling	weather
Mon	Jan May Sep	Today this is me:	Today outside is:
Tue Sat	Feb Jun Oct		
Wed Sun	Mar July Nov		
Thu	Apr Aug Dec		
Fri	____ / 20 ____		

daily doodles

I like to draw. I will draw what I see. Today I saw all that you see.

daily to-do list

Good morning. Today is an awesome day. I have many fun things to do. Let's see!

1
2
3
4
5
6
7
8
9
10
11
12
13
14
15
16
17
18
19
20
21
22
23
24

daily inspiration

Look what I discovered today! So many wonderful things I can do on another day.

to make   to eat   to find

to wear   to remember   to play

to ponder   to create   to see

to be   to visit   to match

daily expenses

Money is good. I work very hard. I want to know where it goes and how far.

Date	Amount	Balance

$5

$30

$3

$150

$200,000

From the brilliant brain of

_____

daily journal

I have many things to write about this day. Just wait until you read what I have to say.

day

Mon
Tue   Sat
Wed   Sun
Thu
Fri

date

Jan	May	Sep
Feb	Jun	Oct
Mar	July	Nov
Apr	Aug	Dec

_____ / 20_____

feeling

Today this is me:

weather

Today outside is:

daily doodles

I like to draw. I will draw what I see. Today I saw all that you see.

daily to-do list

Good morning. Today is an awesome day. I have many fun things to do. Let's see!

1.
2.
3.
4.
5.
6.
7.
8.
9.
10.
11.
12.
13.
14.
15.
16.
17.
18.
19.
20.
21.
22.
23.
24.

daily inspiration

Look what I discovered today! So many wonderful things I can do on another day.

to make   to eat   to find

to wear   to remember   to play

to ponder   to create   to see

to be   to visit   to match

daily expenses

Money is good. I work very hard. I want to know where it goes and how far.

Date	Amount	Balance

$5

$30

$3

$150

$200,000

 From the brilliant brain of

_____

daily journal

I have many things to write about this day. Just wait until you read what I have to say.

day	date	feeling	weather
Mon	Jan May Sep	Today this is me:	Today outside is:
Tue Sat	Feb Jun Oct		
Wed Sun	Mar July Nov		
Thu	Apr Aug Dec		
Fri	____ / 20____		

daily doodles

I like to draw. I will draw what I see. Today I saw all that you see.

daily to-do list

Good morning. Today is an awesome day. I have many fun things to do. Let's see!

1. ○
2. ○
3. ○
4. ○
5. ○
6. ○
7. ○
8. ○
9. ○
10. ○
11. ○
12. ○
13. ○
14. ○
15. ○
16. ○
17. ○
18. ○
19. ○
20. ○
21. ○
22. ○
23. ○
24. ○

daily expenses

Money is good. I work very hard. I want to know where it goes and how far.

Date	Amount	Balance

$5

$30

$3

$150

$200,000

From the brilliant brain of

_____

daily journal

I have many things to write about this day. Just wait until you read what I have to say.

day
Mon
Tue   Sat
Wed   Sun
Thu
Fri

date
Jan   May   Sep
Feb   Jun   Oct
Mar   July   Nov
Apr   Aug   Dec

_____ / 20 _____

feeling
Today this is me:

weather
Today outside is:

daily doodles

I like to draw. I will draw what I see. Today I saw all that you see.

daily to-do list

Good morning. Today is an awesome day. I have many fun things to do. Let's see!

1 _____ O
2 _____ O
3 _____ O
4 _____ O
5 _____ O
6 _____ O
7 _____ O
8 _____ O
9 _____ O
10 _____ O
11 _____ O
12 _____ O
13 _____ O
14 _____ O
15 _____ O
16 _____ O
17 _____ O
18 _____ O
19 _____ O
20 _____ O
21 _____ O
22 _____ O
23 _____ O
24 _____ O

daily inspiration

Look what I discovered today! So many wonderful things I can do on another day.

to make   to eat   to find

to wear   to remember   to play

to ponder   to create   to see

to be   to visit   to match

daily expenses

Money is good. I work very hard. I want to know where it goes and how far.

Date	Amount	Balance

$5

$30

$3

$150

$200,000

From the brilliant brain of

_____

daily journal

I have many things to write about this day. Just wait until you read what I have to say.

day

Mon
Tue   Sat
Wed   Sun
Thu
Fri

date

Jan	May	Sep
Feb	Jun	Oct
Mar	July	Nov
Apr	Aug	Dec

_____ / 20_____

feeling

Today this is me:

weather

Today outside is:

daily doodles

I like to draw. I will draw what I see. Today I saw all that you see.

daily to-do list

Good morning. Today is an awesome day. I have many fun things to do. Let's see!

1 _____ O
2 _____ O
3 _____ O
4 _____ O
5 _____ O
6 _____ O
7 _____ O
8 _____ O
9 _____ O
10 _____ O
11 _____ O
12 _____ O
13 _____ O
14 _____ O
15 _____ O
16 _____ O
17 _____ O
18 _____ O
19 _____ O
20 _____ O
21 _____ O
22 _____ O
23 _____ O
24 _____ O

daily inspiration

Look what I discovered today! So many wonderful things I can do on another day.

to make   to eat   to find

to wear   to remember   to play

to ponder   to create   to see

to be   to visit   to match

daily expenses

Money is good. I work very hard. I want to know where it goes and how far.

Date	Amount	Balance

$5

$30

$3

$150

$200,000

From the brilliant brain of

_____

daily journal

I have many things to write about this day. Just wait until you read what I have to say.

day

Mon
Tue   Sat
Wed   Sun
Thu
Fri

date

Jan   May   Sep
Feb   Jun   Oct
Mar   July   Nov
Apr   Aug   Dec

_____ / 20_____

feeling

Today this is me:

weather

Today outside is:

daily doodles

I like to draw. I will draw what I see. Today I saw all that you see.

daily to-do list

Good morning. Today is an awesome day. I have many fun things to do. Let's see!

1
2
3
4
5
6
7
8
9
10
11
12
13
14
15
16
17
18
19
20
21
22
23
24

daily inspiration

Look what I discovered today! So many wonderful things I can do on another day.

to make   to eat   to find

to wear   to remember   to play

to ponder   to create   to see

to be   to visit   to match

daily expenses

Money is good. I work very hard. I want to know where it goes and how far.

Date	Amount	Balance

$5

$30

$3

$150

$200,000

From the brilliant brain of

_____

daily journal

I have many things to write about this day. Just wait until you read what I have to say.

day

Mon
Tue   Sat
Wed   Sun
Thu
Fri

date

Jan   May   Sep
Feb   Jun   Oct
Mar   July   Nov
Apr   Aug   Dec

_____ / 20 _____

feeling

Today this is me:

weather

Today outside is:

daily doodles

I like to draw. I will draw what I see. Today I saw all that you see.

daily to-do list

Good morning. Today is an awesome day. I have many fun things to do. Let's see!

1. _____ O
2. _____ O
3. _____ O
4. _____ O
5. _____ O
6. _____ O
7. _____ O
8. _____ O
9. _____ O
10. _____ O
11. _____ O
12. _____ O
13. _____ O
14. _____ O
15. _____ O
16. _____ O
17. _____ O
18. _____ O
19. _____ O
20. _____ O
21. _____ O
22. _____ O
23. _____ O
24. _____ O

daily inspiration

Look what I discovered today! So many wonderful things I can do on another day.

to make   to eat   to find

to wear   to remember   to play

to ponder   to create   to see

to be   to visit   to match

daily expenses

Money is good. I work very hard. I want to know where it goes and how far.

Date	Amount	Balance

$5

$30

$3

$150

$200,000

From the brilliant brain of

_____

daily journal

I have many things to write about this day. Just wait until you read what I have to say.

day

Mon
Tue   Sat
Wed   Sun
Thu
Fri

date

Jan   May   Sep
Feb   Jun   Oct
Mar   July   Nov
Apr   Aug   Dec

_____ / 20_____

feeling

Today this is me:

weather

Today outside is: